a rose
arose

qasim chauhan

send & receive more love at

my instagram: @roohdaar

edited by emily maroutian
instagram: @emaroutian

share the *love*

ISBN: 1095430424
ISBN-13: 9781095430422

also check out my first book *qalb*

to everyone who is going through a tough phase, but is still thriving and making efforts to help anyone. this is for you, the practitioner of love.

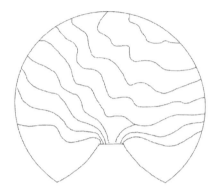

be gentle
with me
i am sweet lava
and an ocean of love

boundaries vanishes
when we love

and
when we love
we understand
everything

one becomes all
all becomes one

everything melts

and when
they understood each other
their symphony
was heard by the multiverse

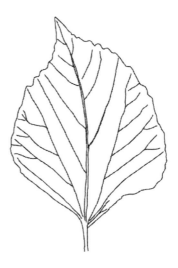

i often
ask people about
the meaning of their names
and call them
by the meaning of it

try it
and
you will learn a lot
in the process
about the person,
self and the languages

- *wānιū*

the way
you compliment someone
says a lot about you
and your awareness
than about them

- *reverse*

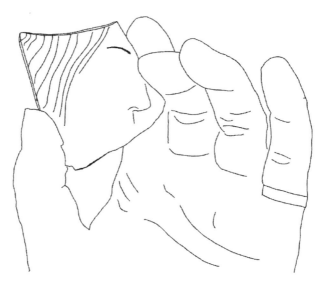

while making your portrait
my brush kept colouring you
in many colours
which you gave me
and now i don't know why
you fear your own shades

- i only showed you a mirror

its just three things
which are most important
when it comes to living life

kindness
honesty
and
integrity

can you please think
before you speak?

because your few words
can give
direction to people

- who are you?
a healer
or the wound?

my masterpiece,
master peace.

that girl
which you mocked for being tomboyish upon seeing her short hair, is actually someone who donates her hair regularly to cancer patients

that girl
whom you find crazy and strangely sensitive is actually someone who has suffered many situations and she survived every time. her scars are her own. she still struggles.

that boy
whom you saw making excellent artworks, she told me about his life. pain was the name of her father and silence was of her mother. no wonder why he has so much to say through art.

that boy
with long hair, he told me about why he sometimes stops cutting his hair. he said whenever he feels like his life is becoming a mess and he needs to work on it while crying, that's when he stops caring about cutting his hair.

that boy
which you mock for stammering was born like that. he has tried several methods to cure it. but recently when he accepted it and worked on his own self. he saw improvements. but your mocking made a relapse in his weeks of work.

that colleague
which you mocked for being overweight. lately, he
struggles a lot with suicidal thoughts, but arose like a
phoenix from it. i wish you spoke kinder.

people are not what they look
and life can be at times difficult
you never know the whole story
so
just be kind please
you will feel peace
when you give
other people peace

fill the ink
wherever you find
an empty pen
and reincarnate it
into a revolution

- *healer*

my pen has witnessed
how
words become actions
pain becomes poetry
efforts become success
hurting disappointments become anger
practice becomes excellence
love becomes revolution
pain becomes art
art becomes poetry
poetry becomes stars
shining in darkness
and singing all along
songs of silence and love

my beloved
if i ever gave you
pain, disappointments
or tears

i will apologize
with the stars and moon
and remind you
how this dusk will
eventually lead us
to a beautiful place
where love is eternal

- *autumn to spring*

my journey
shaped me.
a unique art.

- *snowflake*

we all are
like ores,
full of precious treasure
hidden within everyone

but
*are you working on yourself
or are you just lost in the dust?*

let the pain
change the arrangements
of your carbons
making you a diamond
so that you could reflect
and see
everything within

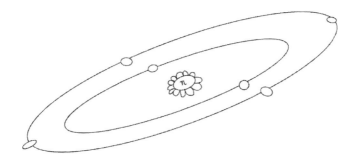

she
stopped explaining herself
when she heard
'*explanation kills art*'

- *feel art and artist*

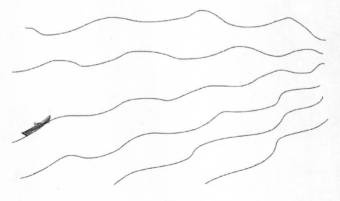

her hair
was the sign
of her fearlessness

her smile
was the sign
of her innocence

and her scars
were the sign
of her boundless freedom

the universe often tells me stories
about the formation of stars

how small dust
gathered
with the passage of time,
perseverance,
and gravity
turns into
stars

have you not yet
heard of this?

come closer
let me whisper it
to you

it is not a battle
of you vs. yourself
stop making wars
with your own self

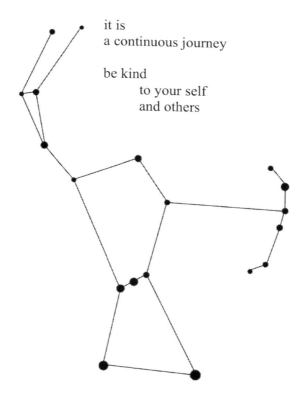

it is
a continuous journey

be kind
    to your self
    and others

the ache of learning more
can never be healed

- *beautiful ache*

love gives you
colours and wings
to fly high and
spread the colour of love
over everyone

- *rangrez*

you don't have to beg
for love to stay
it will flow into your life
and stay forever
without you even asking

- khalis

when my tears
fell on a painting from the past
that was the day
i learned
watercolour painting

- *tears*

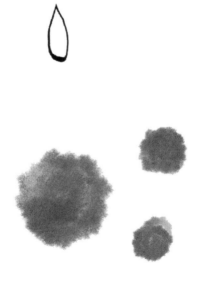

love colours pain
into a painting

- *the canvas of life*

one night
my mind waged a war at my heart
and asked me
did she really love you?

i stammered a bit
but then a train of memories
went right in front of my eyes

- flashback

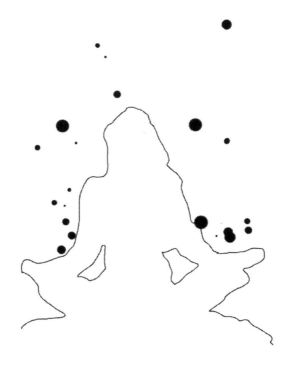

i found you
in everything
in everywhere
i thought
you might not be there

i found you
in middle of chaos
and a twisted pair of love

and
you made me
a calm tornado
a rhythmic and infinite
shower of love

- *i found you here*

do you trust
the universal will?

are you ready
to explore
the universe within?

why do you never call me first?
i have waited for your call many times
past me

i have concluded one thing
if i ever feel like talking
i will call first and
won't wait around for anyone
present me

so you want to talk to her/him
but don't want to call first

what is it?
grow up.

communicate with them
or at least tell them you want her/him to call you too like
you do. make it simple. communicate please.

- self note

yesterday
was painful
but
i knew
you will be mine

- *learning patience*

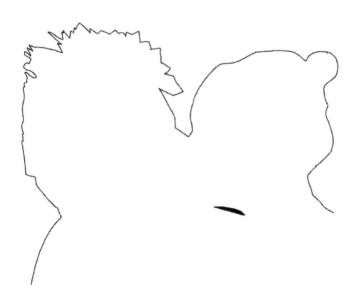

she is
poetry in motion
voicing the silenced
helping everyone
with her gifts

she is
art in progress
forever heartwarming
and reaching beyond

how to believe
in love again
after a breakup?
she asked

visit your parents'
old home
listen to children playing
in a playground
she heard a whisper

connections
are meant to give you freedom
and if you feel bounded, limited
and restricted in it,
its not what you should be in

love gives wings to fly
        roots to stay connected
                to the source
        power to do everything
                with sincerity
        and respect everyone as they are

who said i forgot
some things we can do together?

matching tattoo
paragliding
double cheese corn pizza
lots of hugs and kisses
and rest of life together

these are the reasons
for our next union

- *be mine*

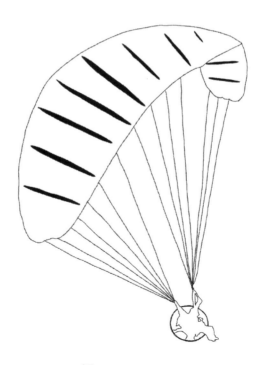

she smiles
every time
she draws

she rises
every time
she cries

she blesses
every time
she touches

she makes fire
every time
everywhere
with her golden heart

- *i saw fire*
  of passion
  and warmth

you made me feel
how love tastes like

- *valdaro lovers*

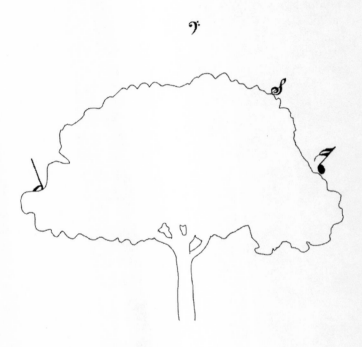

whisper something
really sweet
to yourself
right now

love
embraces everyone
and makes them
so close to themselves
that there is no difference
remaining
between
any duality

*- tight hug of love
  builds bridges of life*

have i not painted
the sky for you
just like you painted
my heart
with honey

i will
unveil the secrets
for you
just don't be
in hurry
to solve
or to conclude

sit
listen
observe
and
see
the magic
unfolding

can i be a light
to myself?

no
they won't understand
your unconditional love
that's why it is *unconditional*
to give them love
without any condition

love is here

i was

i was fond of you
i was in awe
in love

you once were inside my heart

you once were
were

- *was and were*

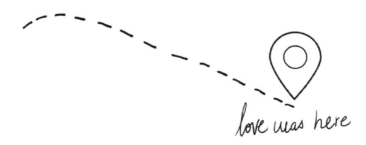

forgive yourself often
forgive yourself a thousand times
and know that
you were not wrong
in loving them so deeply

not all roads
take you to the destination
but have you enjoyed the journey?
      have you learned something?
      are you not wiser than before?

you are
stronger than you think

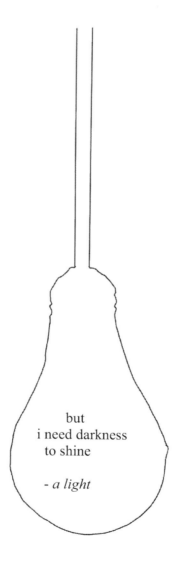

but
i need darkness
to shine

- *a light*

make
your home
a place
where
love lives
lives love

- *foundation*

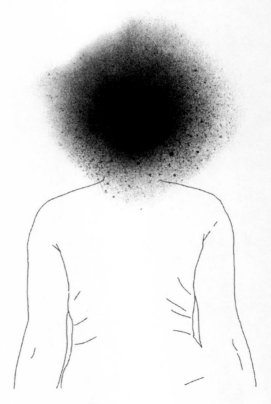

know this
that many people
will come to you
and say about your home

it doesn't look good
it would be better if you used this colour
what are these lines?
it doesn't match with others
why is it so short?
you should try doing this
why didn't you ask me before?
have you seen my house?
they say

just don't listen to them
and realize that you are not them
you are you and that is your power

you don't have to fit in.
create a new world.

- interior designer of the soul

and when
after many setbacks
i found no road
i cried
and cried

i told my tears
to help me
by being a medium
and then i swam across

when you don't give up
the universe performs a miracle
and help comes from
unexpected places

she taught me
the language of love
and
the language of letting go

- she was a beautiful disaster

and she kept
another secret
inside her

i saw how
her whole garden of flowers
turned into darkness

- *her silent screams make me deaf*

she was fascinated
by fire and how it burns

i still remember
her favourite phrase
i love fire
it fills my oceans

attachment: some people think i am not good and have very bad affect, but little do they know about me. it is very important to be attached to people, and your passion. that is what keeps you going in life when you see yourself attached to something larger than yourself – a dream. but you must know when to stop. take control of yourself and your life.

love: most of the time people just limit me to just romantic relationships. actually they haven't seen or tasted real love. love which is universal and has no limit. love which will make you fearless and joyous. when you feel this kind of love, you will feel connected to your beloved as much as any other thing. of course romantic relations exist, but so does love in many other ways.

she was
made of
love
passion
patience
fire
and
gratitude

the secrets
of her existence
smile within her

love will find you
and make you bloom

meanwhile
be patient enough and
water your garden of soul
with self love
to bloom within first

love will find you
and make you bloom
more than ever before

- *together*

i choose love
even after an argument

listen and
love

i am an empath
i choose love

- *mutual*

she
was unstoppable
when she realized
herself
her power

and
promised
i will raise
a revolution

- *legacy*

but
sometimes
i only wish
for more pain
cause
it stays

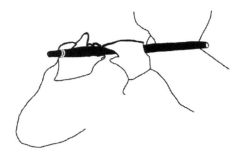

i kissed my wounds
last night
they tasted like
painful unacceptance

so
i kissed my wounds again
and poured my love on them

and then
i kissed my wounds again
they are now my strength

- *three kisses*

i know
i am broken
but i want love
not your pity

- *worth*

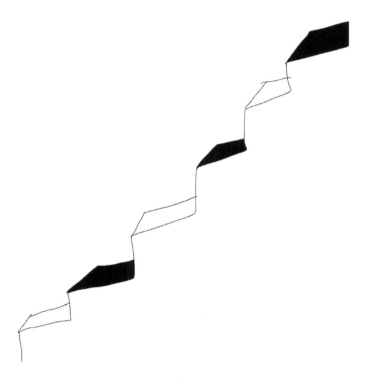

i went to the park yesterday
to have some refreshing time
and the little child
whispered in my ear
why are you not playing?

i am tired, dear
i replied

you know
i never get tired
because i love
the child said

i felt those words
deep within me

don't you love playing?
the child asked

- rest, not quit

there is so much
out there
waiting for you
to explore

once you stop
judging and
start travelling
within and
the world
you will be
another being
altogether

- *to be continued*

i will keep
this within me
but
i won't
give up;

i choose life

- semi colon;

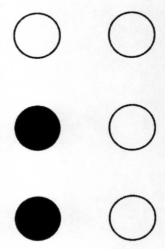

is it right to sacrifice
my happiness for others?
asked someone from the crowd

if you do
either you are a *dar'wish*
or someone who just shows off
or a person who is naive and
not aware of it

because
it is not an easy task
it takes so much effort
and energy to process
but over time
you will become
a powerful soul

you don't have to
but it is very precious
if you do it

continuously remind yourself
about your dreams
and purpose

- *breathe*

a blessing of
understanding
and feeling everyone
comes with
a curse of
understanding

you can love everyone
if you understand
and
for the same reason
you can't hate anyone

even the people
who gave you pain
are the tragic stories

it's tiring at times
but
keep your health in check
and keep filling
your cup of self love

with her
i feel i will never
be able to
thank her enough
for all the happiness
and
memories
we shared

you are
a poem
which the universe
wrote with love.

- mother

qasim chauhan

i hide myself
beneath
waterfalls
stones
fascination
art
atoms
wisdom
intellect

but
all that
you see
in all these creations
is your own self
just in different
material form

there is so much
fun
in hide and seek

- *god to humans. one.*

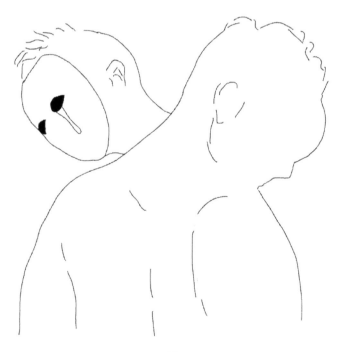

do
what makes
you uncomfortable
that's how a seed
grows into a forest

- jump

and
we matched
like the last pieces
of a puzzle

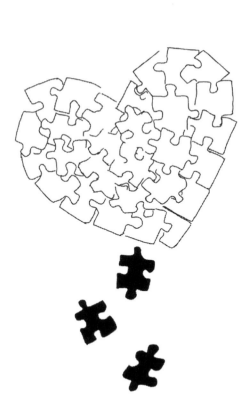

love is when
understanding marries respect

- *marriage*

a rose arose

lakhs of words
still lack of
understanding

- texting

i haven't seen
anything more beautiful
than a strong person
smiling in pain

their teary eyes
narrate a story of
how they calmed
the storm with
their heart
and a smile

the efforts
they give to make
others happy
while they themselves
are in pain
makes them
the sweetest and
most beautiful

when she was leaving
for the airport
i picked a yellow colour
and touched her with it
giving her another
yellow warm memory

the day has come, the day of separation and the day
when love feels warmest and closest to our heart. my
sister was packing her family's clothes when my father
noticed that she forgot the shoes. perhaps she listened
yesterday when my father was said *'we will keep
lucman's shoes with us'* in memory of his innocence.
memory, a small six letter word but the whole world
revolves around it. it is only the memories which make
us. aren't we all just mere collections of memories
through different set of paths? while my father kept the
shoes of my nephew, i took the yellow colour which i
touched her with before. it was kept near the mirror,
quite an unexpected place but she knew i will see there
as i played with lucman near the mirror. she left both
things for us and went on her journey. all this i once
thought was just coincidence but i am sure she planned it
like this and it happened.

- *i love you*

i am
a precious life
as much as everyone else

*- be kind to all species
be humble*

your message
is the sunshine
which
gives me
warmth

and
the last thing
she told me
was
pain
is addictive

sometimes
the children
playing in the playground
gives you a deeper and
more refreshing perspective
to see the world
with less seriousness
and with more enjoyment

are you enjoying
the life you are living?

since he loved her
she never felt
as much freedom
like this before
and she told me
i feel much closer
to myself

his love has ignited
the spark in her
of fearless passion
and pure bliss

the way you love me
is as if all my prayers
are answered
and
i am home

i am
just here
learning
and
making
memories

if there exists
a phenomenon of incarnation
i would love to become a woman
in my next birth

i want to know
how it feels to
live in a country
where a goddesses are
prayed to daily and
simultaneously
people behave
very wrong to women

i still wonder
how can people forget
a woman gave you birth
but now you are
scarring their soul

- *last wish*

your love is as pure
and as meaningful
as someone living
far away from you

love is a feeling
which has no language
and through it
deaf and blind
can hear and see
and even thorns
turn into flowers

your memories and
efforts together
make it special
for you

i want to be her water
when she bathes.
warm and soothing.

- *all over her*

i fear how it will end
he said

i wonder will it even end
she said and kissed him

we see reflection
of ourselves in other things
and call them *god*

- *oh know*

each breathe
reminds me of you
oh beloved
you live in between two

- *new home*

and
she gave me the reason
to use the word *'always'*
more often

- *trust*

i am clouds
and
you are rays
together
we play
the game
of shadow
and
do art in the sky

but how do i know
that i love her?
random person asked

put a hand on your heart
close your eyes
and think of
all the memories
you have had

did this make you
smile and shine
and
give you *sukoon*?

you will now
know the answer

loudness
is not confidence
but
calmness is

controlling
others
is not care
but
listening
to their dream is

everyone
and
everything
teaches
if
you have
the burning desire
to learn

my loneliness asked me
why are you not
a good friend
with your own self?

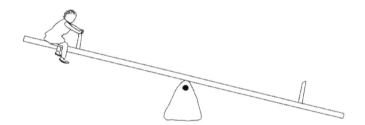

be your own medicine
be your own cure
heal your wounds
embrace your uniqueness
and
keep spreading
the message of love

till death
we do love

- nine lives for *art*

love turns
adjective
and verb
into noun

- *beautiful*
  cutie pie
  love

consumerism
turns noun
into a verb

- *google it*

my heart beats
just like you
and i too have the same blood
just like you
but you separate
me and make me
feel like
i am nothing

i bleed red
i feel love
i cry poetry
and
i have been broken too

 - *lgbtq*

when i cried
it rained but
i concealed the tears
with a smile
and that was how
every rainbow
was born

- *love is love*

your colours
are unique
and
when
you shine
you become
a midnight rainbow

- to everyone reading this

whenever
i do selfless acts
i replace my pride
with the flower of humbleness
and now
i have become
a garden
where
we all play

when i arose in love
it was like seeds of love
got the warmth of sun rays
and photosynthesis
painted my whole
existence into
a garden of flowers

there will be
some people
who just visit flowers
to cut them for their
temporary pleasure.
possession is
the only way to love.
they think.

but the magic happens
when someone comes
with good intentions
to water the plant
embrace all of it
be with it
to know
and feel
all the seasons
with it

it hurts
to the core
knowing
that we are losing
the depth of words

maa
aachaar
awaaz
inquilaab
parvaaz
khwaab
gharonda

- learn languages
but don't let
your native language
become an orphan

words
are powerful

use them
with care

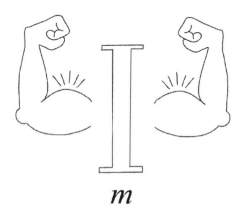

how wonderful
was it
when you understood
my infinite
love for myself

- *fractals*

thank you
for understanding
me

- *fibonacci sequence*
  to golden ratio

your eyes hold me
tighter and warmer
than hundreds of hugs

your voice shines up
my heart
like sun shines up
the moon

your smell
with mine

- *intimacy*

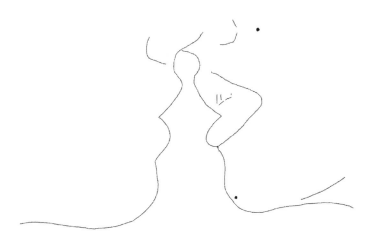

i tried a lot
to paint her
but wasn't able to
paint the exact features
of her beauty

suddenly
i experienced something
that changed my life
i started forgetting
but i didn't stop painting her

than one day
a miracle happened
i painted her
i could see her there
on my canvas
as beautiful as she is

that day i came to realize
how accidents have
the power to create and
destroy worlds

- *accidental abstract*

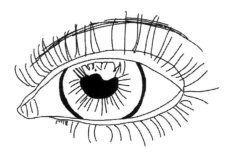

i loved
the glow of your soul
of innocence
kindness
playfulness
rawness
and purity

i used to know a girl
who once loved 'memories'
and 'yellow colour'

but sadly
her memory wasn't her friend
and she started forgetting

little did i know
but last time i saw her
she showed me her new paintings
which she used to call
by her own name

- *you are your memories*

and it is only through pain
love is born

- *yin and yang*

he used to call himself chaos
maybe he has not seen love yet
maybe he lied when he spoke of reasons for scars
maybe he has been through something painful
maybe he fails not because he is not studying but
because he is not able to study at home
maybe he wasn't only misunderstood but also mistreated
maybe his dark circles were the sign of sleepless nights
maybe his screams were silenced each time
with power

i cry often
just realizing how
he use to sit in playground
and no one cared

only if anyone of us
heard his screams
he could be saved

- *domestic violence*

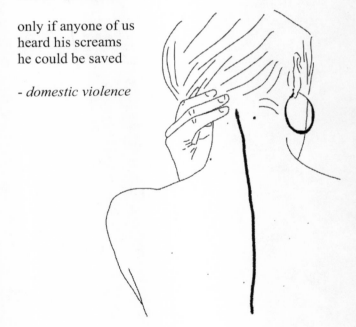

maybe someday scars will heal
but what about the memories
which will haunt for years

will they ever be healed?

i once drank her tears
they tasted like weeping storms
desiring to be known
and loved

i once drank her tears
they tasted like a mystical answer
to all my questions

i once drank her tears
they tasted like my mother's pure love
i could feel the emotions and warmth
in them

- *more than just tears*

i miss you like all the good events
that are yet to happen in my life

i miss you like
a canvas misses the colours
to be poured on it

i miss you like
sunflowers miss
the sun at night

- *prepone*

your memories
never stopped
blooming flowers
and giving me
the fragrance of love

- *day after another*

what's wrong with having expectations?

is it wrong to expect love and respect
after giving my soul and body to you?

is it wrong to expect?

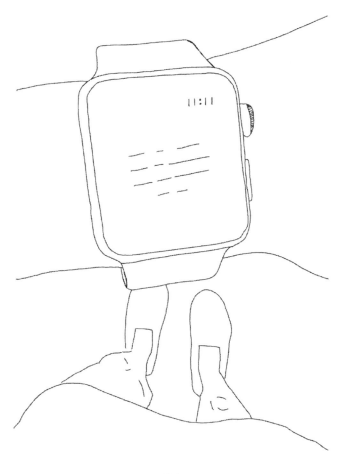

when
all you do
is just listen to others
try to fit in
blend yourself
as per environment
you will never
know your true self
and
will disappear.

- *chameleon*

support your friends
like you do celebrities
or other famous people

support them
by
listening to their dreams
giving them feedback
buying their product
reading their book
sharing it with others

- *spread the love*

in solving the equation of life
and unveiling its mysteries
you, my silly friend,
have forgotten its
endless experiences of joy
simplicity, innocence
and taste of the unknown.

- you are life

she is mine, mine
the treasure i love
the treasure i adore
the treasure which
made me treasure

she is mine, mine
a raw source
of infinite supply
of love

- *queen*

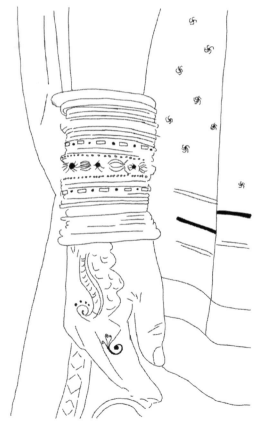

drop
all the '*be*'s
and just **be.**

- *listen yourself*

bye
i will miss you too
and your warmth
but
i've got to do
magic with
passion

- *comfort zone*

we travelled
the world and
grew old together
and
i love how she smiles
and that smile
echoes in the mountains
of my heart
for eternity

earth
is our home

warmth is
our language

love is
our religion

- remember this earthlings

close your eyes
to see

- *your mirror*

mirrors
don't get
fixed easily

- *broken*

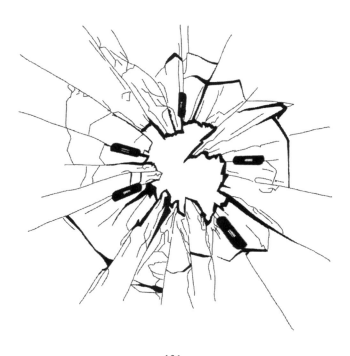

probably
the last sunset
will make you realize
the meaningfulness
of the gifts of nature

- *do something before it's too late*

to love
is to celebrate
uniqueness
and flaws equally

- *grow*

you understand me
give me goosebumps
make me smile
and
the most precious
is the way
you make an effort
for us

- *marry me*

when you touched
me with your warmth
all my worries, anger
and pain
melted into
peaceful water
for my soul

- *rooh*

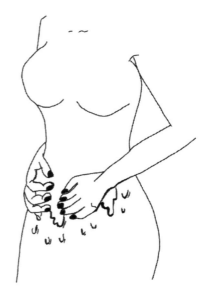

some people
were admirers
of her coldness

but he saw
the reason behind it
and rolled her into
a journey of self love

- *ice cream*

tears
are my
language

- *depression*

i remember
she used to keep painting herself
in the colours of the moon and sun together

her soul brightens both
the day and the night

- *full moon*

volumes
of wisdom
are hidden within
everything

to understand
the universe
observe nature
and self

- *oneness*

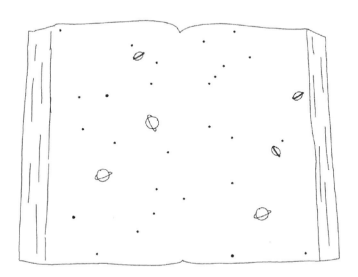

when she showed me
her childhood pictures

i was amazed to see such a cutie
and i just felt like
there is something which connects us both

i know i haven't met her before
or saw her childhood pictures
but i somehow felt
i am connected
to her and
her memories

i feel her
within me

- smiling tears told me to write this

these tears are precious.
listen them, embrace them,
love them, kiss them,
make them feel better,
know them, and in knowing,
you'll find a teacher, a friend,
a mirror and infinite love.
tears water our
understanding of life.

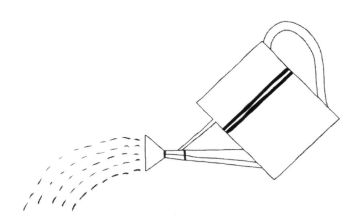

what is the difference between
passion and addiction?

passion is
a healthy
self-driven journey
and
addiction is
is driving blindfolded
where you can hurt
yourself and others too

the last storm
destroyed me
but
the storm
you are in now
is the one that
will make you
change things
and push you out
of your comfort zone
to build
a home with
dreams in vision

i remember
how she used to whisper
thank you, teacher
to her pain
and happiness

- *gratitude*

sometimes
a person is
in peace
and in pieces
simultaneously

- *hidden pain*

dear heart
why are you still nice
to all these bad people?
reasoning asked

they need love
and i am just a messenger
giving them what they need most
heart answered

kindness
is the most precious
virtue
and a sign of
a strong person

imperfection
isn't imperfection,

it's just
uniqueness
misnamed.

flute,
soap bubbles,
stars and
your touch;

everything
what i need.

what are your qualities?

are you true to yourself?

do you feel healthy
and happy doing what you do?

use space on next page to write a message which resonates with your dream goal. refer the page or paste it somewhere a rose arose

qasim chauhan

don't listen
to people labeling you
in various things
you know
who you are and
your intentions

what makes life
more meaningful?
i asked buddhu

pain and death
buddhu replied

when you are looking for
only pretty faces
you will never
be at peace

but when you look for
love and good intentions
you will feel
peace

- *contentment*

qasim chauhan

you are a song
which i long singing
and
a poem
which i love reading

he named
her daughter
geet
in the memory
of his beloved
ghazal

kiss her
stretch marks
and her scars
the way you
kiss her forehead

- *respect*

she gave birth
to love and thunder
revolution and a blessing
happiness and joy

- *twins*

there is no *way*
to attain happiness

it originates
within
when one realizes
the love

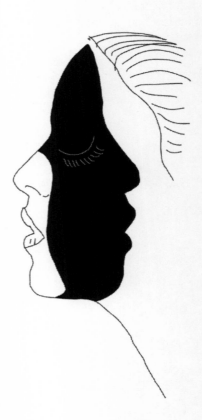

we never felt close enough
even though our skins were touching
because
what desire and love
we have for each other
can only be satisfied
with the closeness of years together
with our souls dancing
with our lips overflowing poetry
with our eternal love
with our understanding
with our non-vocal conversations
with our eye talk
with our loyalty
with our pure intentions

- *we are love*

can you tell me
where do i play?

tell me a place
where my freedom isn't questioned

tell me a place
where i am not suppressed

tell me a place
where i am not told to be silent

tell me a place
where i am not stopped when laughing loudly

- tell me a place

i have no place
to play

all these vultures
are eating my innocence
and replacing it
with fear and darkness

i wonder
how they became so heartless
that they didn't feel my pain

i just have a wish
for once you feel my pain
i assure you
you'll never be unkind to anyone

i stopped playing
and started existing
and at times
i question why i'm even alive

- *let me breath*

whenever
i have no word
to express my feelings
*i utter **i love you***
with my tearful eyes
he said

i wonder
what is more deep
your tearful eyes
or the words you uttered
she said

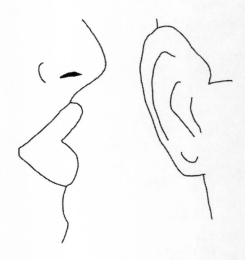

and when death will come,
will you be happy for the choices
you have made
and memories you had with people?

qasim chauhan

you won't be happy
by making others feel sad

- *temporary*

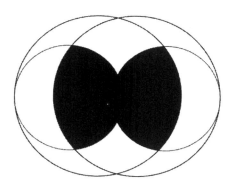

soon
we will be birds
and
we will fly together

- *wings of fire*

many people
just see the light
but a few know
about the burning
of the sun

we enjoy
the music
of the flute
and drum
but a few know
about the pain
of their scars

we see great
poets, writers
but a few know
the mess and chaos
they have inside them

many people see
the light of the sun
but a few do know
the story of fire
which is within her
all along

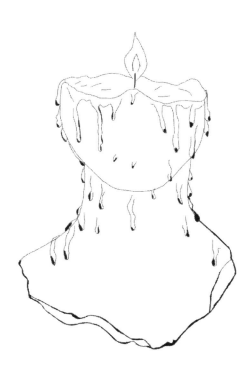

i am nowhere to be found
but within
and the way to find me
is 'not to find me'
happiness told me

why does
the effect of
bad words
stay longer
than
the effect of
compliments?

- don't give power to anyone
  to make you go insane

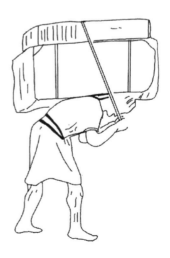

i am sleepless nights
and a night owl

- *waiting*

all addictions are
a form of self harm
where you divert your
pain from present moment
but soon all this diversion
becomes an infinite never-ending tunnel
and you get lost in it

- *t minus 21 days*

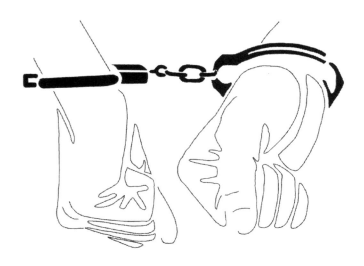

romantic days

kiss

i love you more
than anything
in this world
he said

she said **no**
and rejected
his proposal

how come you
say that
i hate you more
than anything
in this world
he said

sixteen stabs

do you know
how avalanches
form

when water vapors
convert directly
from gas to solid
the most beautiful
'stellar dendrite'
becomes prime reason
for it

heal others
to heal yourself

i write
i cry oceans
i roar rainbows

- *vulnerability*

she wears black
because
she is full of colours

- *literally within*

i might be angry
but will remain silent
and cry alone by myself
instead of
fighting with you
for some respect

- *you will notice if i matter to you*

how's your beloved?
people asked while mocking

the universe is wonderful
and so is she
i replied with a smile

but what.....what if?
she stopped her question
halfway but he knew
what she wanted to ask

if we would not be together
i won't search for you anywhere
for you will live along my breathe
and remembered every second

- *you know it, right?*

sita + kabir
they met
fell in love
but couldn't
marry
because of
religion

years passed

both met
accidentally
but again couldn't
marry
because of
religion
made them
shaheen + krishan

who knew
their souls
were married
and never
separated

- *purest love story*

i grew with my plants
soft life, enchanting beauty
and thriving on sunlight
and moonlight

- *gamla and chakora*

shades of outer shell
can't describe
the inner light
what you are
is indescribable

- *soul of soul of love*

once there was a girl
who didn't know how
to say 'no'
and she took everything
way too seriously

and then came one man
who told her how
to say 'no' and what
we see now
is that she even said
'no' to that man

he abused her
and harmed himself

- *please heal yourself first*

you fear new love
because it wasn't well last time
just be patient and stick around me
and i promise you will witness
a love that lasts for eternity
and would be *sukoonful*

- *i yellow you*

you don't know yourself
allow me to be your mirror
cause
you don't know yourself

let me remind you of the days
the days which
were heavier than mountains
and it seemed hard to walk
but look at yourself
you have gone through all of that
with love and power

let me remind you of the days
the days which
seemed like
never ending darkness
but look at yourself
look how brightly you shine
with grace and art

let me remind you of the days
the days which
you chose to love yourself
more than anything
that was the day
you took your power back
from other people

let me remind you of the days
the days you
made your first art
and started making memories
it was a journey of ups and downs
but that's what the life is
full of everything,
something
and nothing

let me tell you of the days
the days which
you will smile
seeing how buddhu you are
and that day we both will giggle together

meanwhile
you don't know yourself
allow me to become your mirror
cause
you don't know yourself

- *beautiful dear*

too much of anything
is not good for you
and even a little of
snake venom
can be beneficial

- *you have the power*

am i burden to you?

so you want to leave me because
you think it will be like last time
but do you not see the difference
of the way i love you

so you want to leave me because
you think it would be easier for us
but instead it would be
even more difficult for us

if you think
you don't give me enough time or attention
i can understand that and adjust it
accordingly but leaving because of that
is not the way

if you are tired, relax, rest
and sleep
take care please

letters danced
with joy when
i wrote the title of a poem
it was her name

they started chatting
'this is such a sweet
combination of words'
'we feel happy
as you gathered'

the poem i wrote ended
but the word keeps
coming and saying to me
can you please
write a book for
her? we want
to make our
happy world
where words
have meaning

i
was told
to be a healing balm
for self and others
by the morning breeze

love
can happen in a moment
but movements and revolutions
can occur
when it's true at its core

you
are deeper than oceans
and sweater than honey
oh beloved
never stop being kind

i am flower
who knows
its power

we are
born

       through love
       to love
       by love

how can we be anything
but love

be patient
it takes its own time
for one to realize it

- the journey of self-realization

just tell me
why am i
not in the story?

- *loyalty and clarity*

you are
as much a teacher
as much a student
of life
and love

would you be
my moon
whom i can gaze
for eternity
and admire
its presence?

would you be
my sun
who gives me
the warmth
in divine proportion
from afar?

would you be
my memory
of the past
which is valuable
to me but
i am trying
to forget it?

- *three ways to love*

are you the love
you are desiring
or
are you just demanding it?

- be what you desire
be ready to see the mirror

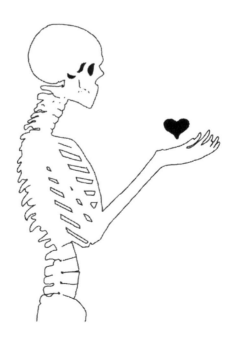

we are *a medium*
that amplifies love
and eliminates hatred

a medium
that feels too much
yet remains calm

a medium
which has gone through chaos
but still speaks of love

- *zariya*

i own nothing
and no one owns me

i am everything
and i feel the universe within

i am somewhere
between nothing and everything

what are you wearing today honey
he softly whispered

i am wearing the smile you gave me
with the confidence i had already
along with lots of self love polka dots
she smiles while blooming

your smiling face
is the prettiest flower
i ever saw

- *serene*

some people are like the sun
shining and spreading light

some people are like the moon
reflecting light and love

and while others are like
shooting stars,
who even after they've gone for years
still have influence on us

- *some legends are recognized*
  after their death
  because they are ahead of time

moon was her soap
sun was her shampoo
no doubt she was
the brightest and
warmest hue
of love

my father
you don't know
why i always ride my bike very slow
when you sit behind me

it's....it's just
i want us to talk
and that is the only
time when we talk

you are precious to me
i know we both cry at night
sometimes for our sins
sometimes for love
sometimes in pain

i wish to write letters to you
i wish many things
i have fear within me
you have hesitation
or don't know how
how to speak from your heart

sometime i feel complete failure
as i try to connect and heal others
but what about my own bonds
which are falling or fallen apart already
i am not perfect
neither saint nor what others think
i am just as much chaos as others
accept me as i am

please love
hate won't give
inner peace
and
without
inner peace
you won't
ever be
calm

- *calmness is the first step*

live as if nothing is yours
be as if you are everything

can you really
understand and perceive
something absolutely
because
perception is the boundary
we give to certain things

even my definition
can be different than yours

you are a magical treasure
waiting for the spell
to open it
but you forgot
you are magical treasure
you have the key within

self love is the key

cultivate
good intentions

harvest
soulful connections

i painted a painting
with my words
while missing you
and
if you could hear
you should hear
each colour
each stroke
is calling your name
they want to meet you too

my colours
want to touch you
and
feel your warmth

- *missed one*

ਜਦੋਂ ਇਨਸਾਨ ਨੂੰ ਜ਼ਿਆਦਾ ਹੀ ਕਾਹਲੀ ਹੁੰਦੀ ਏ
ਤਾਂ ਉਹ ਕਈ ਵਾਰ ਜ਼ਿਆਦਾ ਹੀ ਜਲਦੀ ਪਹੁੰਚ ਜਾਂਦਾ ਏ
ਉੱਥੇ ਜਿੱਥੇ ਉਹ ਜਾਣਾ ਨਹੀਂ ਚਾਹੁੰਦਾ ਹੁੰਦਾ

ਜ਼ਿੰਦਗੀ ਕਹਿੰਦਾ ਕੋਈ ਦੌੜ ਏ
ਕਿ ਤੁਸੀਂ ਭੱਜੀ ਜਾਣਾ
ਸਗੋਂ ਇਹ ਤਾਂ
ਸੋਚ ਦੀ ਮੌਜ ਦੀ
ਖੁਸ਼ੀਆਂ ਦੀ ਗ਼ਮਾਂ ਦੀ
ਰਸਤਿਆਂ ਦੀ ਉਲਝਣਾਂ ਦੀ
ਇਕ ਖਾਸ ਜਗ੍ਹਾ ਹੈ
ਜਿਥੇ ਵੱਖ ਵੱਖ ਲੋਗ ਏ

ਕਾਹਲੀ ਨਾ ਕਰ
ਕਾਹਦੀ ਕਾਹਲੀ ਕਰ ਰਿਹਾ ਤੂੰ?
ਮੈਂ ਤੈਨੂੰ ਇਕ ਗੱਲ ਦੱਸਾਂ
ਕਾਹਲੀ ਨਾਲ ਕੰਮ ਪੂਰਾ ਹੋ ਸਕਦਾ ਏ
ਪਰ ਮੁਕੰਮਲ
ਤੇ ਵਾਹ ਮੁਕੰਮਲ
ਨਹੀਂ ਹੋ ਸਕਦਾ
ਉਹਦੇ ਲਈ ਦਿਲ ਦੀ ਜਰੂਰਤ ਹੋਵੇਗੀ
ਤੇ ਦਿਲ ਆਰਾਮ ਨਾਲ ਤੇ ਸਮਝਕੇ ਕੰਮ ਕਰਦਾ ਹੈ

ਜੋ ਕਾਹਲੀ ਵਿਚ ਹੁੰਦੇ ਨੇ
ਉਹ ਅਕਸਰ ਪਹਿਲਾ ਹੀ ਦੇਰ ਜਾਂ ਲੇਟ ਹੁੰਦੇ ਨੇ
ਤੇ ਜਿਹੜੇ ਸਮਝ ਲੈਂਦੇ ਨੇ ਕਿ ਕਾਹਲੀ ਨਹੀਂ
ਸਗੋਂ ਕੰਮ ਇੰਝ ਕਰਨਾ ਚਾਹੀਦਾ ਕਿ ਦਿਲ ਨੂੰ ਖੁਸ਼ੀ ਮਿਲੇ
ਉਹ ਹਮੇਸ਼ਾ ਸਮਝਕੇ ਚੱਲਦੇ ਨੇ

what is real?
he asked

real is a four letter word
spelled as 'love'

make gratitude
your best friend
and
creativity
your muse
and
love
your journey
and
mistakes
your teacher
and
pain
your messenger
and
smiles
your radiator

there are some battles
which you can only win
by not battling or
sometimes even by losing

i kept everything i liked
saved it and hoarded it
like a thing to be kept within my reach
but you were the one who
i liked. i loved. but still.
still i kept you free. and wild.
free as bird. fearless feathers.
floating for forever freely.
and free from every shell.

she taught me
to love is not to possess something
or keep it safely hidden from others
rather
to love is to love
to love is to cut all attachments
yet remain deeply in love with everything

- *love is revolution reincarnated*

should i keep over-loving you
or should i stop?

i feel
i don't know when to stop
not sure
i am not able to measure
the love and limit it

one thing i am sure of
i will not deviate from
the path of love

my love will over-flow
and can sometime keep you
away from me
but eventually i know
this water will cleanse us
empower our connection
and
water our roots

i have seen
my father crying
my mother falling
and witnessed the rise
of the soft sun shining
and giving me warmth

you have seen my fall
wait and see
how i rise

- note to self

she gave birth and
reared roaring rainbows

from her
universe came
into a play

- *bow down to*
  the divine feminine energy

i am you
and
you are me

i love you
the way
i love me

- billions of species

every fighter is not a warrior
but every warrior is a fighter

don't know what is more painful
to feel everything so deeply
or to not feel anything at all

the door is knocking continuously
are you ready to open and
give your dreams the wings they need?

- *qalb*

protect your softness,
this very kindness
of yours,
soft as corolla
and precious sun,
is
the soul of the soul
of universe.

why do people who
never do harm to others
suffer?

why does a small child
keep falling again
and again

- *to learn.*
  to grow.

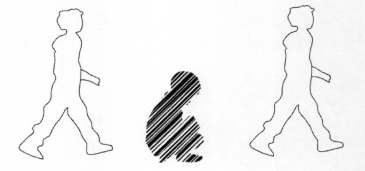

why do people take
advantage of kind people?
asked a person

why do people take
water from a well?
buddhu replied

but you have the choice.
either to let people have water.
or cover yourself.

yesterday is tomorrow
sorry for being late
but here i am now

you are life. just like everyone.
and once you realized that, you will be free of anxiety,
fear and suffering. you will start seeing yourself in
others and others in yourself.

some people see battles
i see unloved people
fighting themselves for love

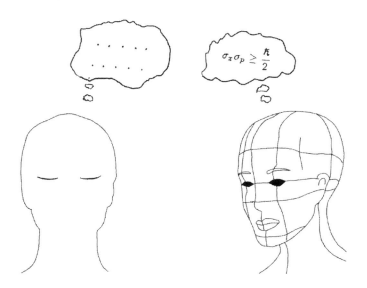

what's your gift
he asked

i transform pain into power
she said

what's your gift
she asked

i can smile while crying
and heal even when i'm broken
he said

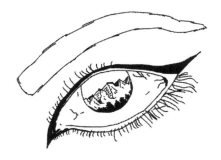

you have no idea
how much love and life
you deserve

can i just stay here
with you for a while
till my last breath
maybe then
you'll understand
you deserve it
every single time
maybe then
we'll understand
the power of true love

my words got tired
of convincing you
so they stopped
shaping into a voice
and became silence

- *before the storm*

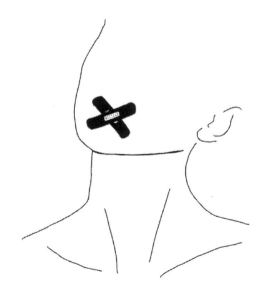

he came running
running towards me
crying. crying. and
repeating the same sentence
again and again
*"there is no one bad
in this world..."*

*"if you give them time
and understand them,
know their pain is
the reason..."*

*"i'm not saying
it's fine what they do.
it's just no one is bad
it's just the circumstances
and how we pave our road
using our love and pain"*

- *buddhu*

i am not perfect
but i love
and those who love
are beyond perfection

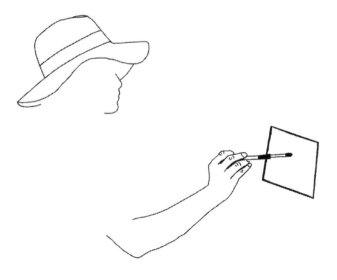

over-caring is limiting.
being silent because
you will probably hurt
the feelings of your beloved
will actually hurt you more
than you ever imagined and
then they'll tell you
that you didn't say anything
so you don't care about us

she once made me feel
i don't know a single bit
about what love is
or how to love

- *falling apart*

qasim chauhan

not feeling
is a feeling too
like an empty heart
we know we need soul food

- *love was here*

love is the second name of revolution
and middle name of unity

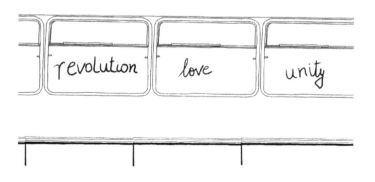

may you get the strength to go through tough days so that you can see your true potential and get the love and blessings you deserve. keep shining.

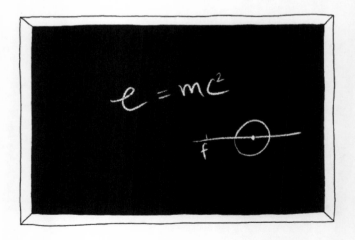

it's okay to be confused
at times
cause
if we solved it all now
what would be the fun?
wouldn't that make life
dull and quite predictable?

embrace the unknown
accept it
and work on it one by one
don't hurry to live your life

i hurt
i grow

i grow
i heal

may you receive the love and happiness you are giving
selflessly to others

dear love. stop taking life so seriously, when you overthink something you miss the joy. do things in life with love and passion, and enjoy the precious moments which won't come again. you can do wonders, just do it now. please.

you are
a melody of uniqueness,
travelling through the multiverse.
realize your potential.

- *know thyself*

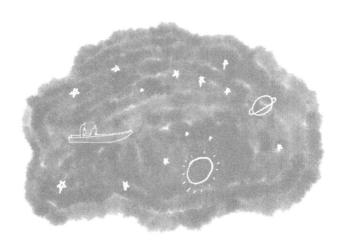

don't feel bad
in feeling too much,
this pure heart
of yours is
the reason why
many people still
believe in
the goodness
and purity of love

it's not i who chose love,
it's the love that chose me
and since then
we choose each other.

- *we*

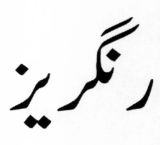

rang'rez

**a dyer. a spiritual
teacher who pour
his colours
(wisdom) and help
them.**

kha'lis

**pure. impeccable.
truth.**

qasim chauhan

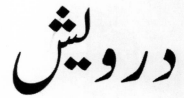

der'wish

**a traveler who is rich
with wisdom and go
door to door to
awaken people.
('der' means door)**

250

sukoon

**peace of mind.
contentment.**

qasim chauhan

ai

love

par'vana

**a moth. a poet.
a lover.**

qasim chauhan

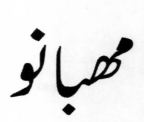

mah'banu

moon lady

sab maya hai

**everything is an
illusion. 'maya'
means illusion.**

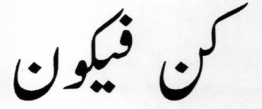

kun faya kuun

be and it is.

saaqi

**literally meaning 'wine
provider' but used as a
metaphor in poetry for
lover, friend, or even god.**

qasim chauhan

258

please stop turning around
and just hold this mirror.

see yourself.
see the universe.
see the unseen.

wa

peace.
harmony.

happiness

happiness is harmony personified. harmony between what we say and what we do. the beautiful thing about happiness is that is not bound to any string, and on the contrary when you bind it with something then life can be very much in pain and exhausted. happiness is something which we all desire and keep searching for endlessly everywhere but happiness is something that you don't have to find.

but where is happiness? happiness is in gratitude. when you wake up in the morning and feel worried about the day coming. turn to gratitude. be thankful of how your body is working, thankful of how far you have come despite all the difficulties and be thankful that you have connections and friends. our connections and friends are a precious wealth. it is together we can do so much for our earth and people in need.

but why does happiness not stay forever? let me put this question in another perspective, *why doesn't it always rain? or why doesn't the sun always shine?* too much of everything can be harmful and also when something is in too much quantity it loses its preciousness. the value of a diamond and charcoal are different because diamonds are less in numbers even though both are quite similar chemically. change is a universal law and everything is temporary. once you realized this you will understand that happiness should not be attached to any string rather let it depend on your own self. smile because you are life. smile because you a are part of this wonderful universe. spread your happiness to double it.

qasim chauhan

改善

kai'zen

**continuous
improvement**

let it go

holding something that doesn't want to stay can be very painful. we all have been through a time when life seems like a burden and no other choice is visible. when life seems to be going out of control. well at that time, it is better to let go of the things you are holding. let go of the need to control everything and feel the situation. it is very important to understand that life is full of ups and downs, and we have to go through it while accepting what comes, and at same time letting go of what or who doesn't want to stay. we can't force things or people to be in certain manner. we shouldn't.

i thought i found the one, but we are not together. there are so many dimensions and angles that sometimes it becomes tiring and one become hopeless. we feel as if we won't ever find the love we desire and need.

the one you are finding won't be some magical person who will transform your life as you kiss them. rather the transformation is usually destructive. one realize that the old buildings must shatter to pieces if we want to build new homes there. the one that you are finding will be a person who does things with love, makes mistakes but apologize, communicates with clarity, cares about you and make continuous efforts for the well being of you both. and you have to be like that too for so that the love multiplies.

qasim chauhan

irusu

**pretending to be out or
not at home when
someone comes by
your house.**

264

time

i am waiting for the right time to begin and when it will be the right time i will do magic. we all feel like this that there might be some sign or that some right time will come which will tell you when to start something. but the right time depends entirely on you. you can use this very paragraph as a sign to start something you wanted start for a while.

the only time limit is that your time on earth is limited. and when you understand that, you will be unstoppable. you will live a thousand of memories in a day and enjoy the happiness of the world in few moments. there is no limit to your powers, take your time to prepare for something and do it when you are prepared. of course there are some things which take their own time, like nature, but no one is stopping you from writing a novel at 56 or teaching at 94. you have limitless powers and there is enough time to live your life in abundance. with love.

don't fall into the trap of 'hurrying,' you don't have to do the things they tell you to. *you are ___ years old and you still don't have this or you can't do that, have you seen your age?* all such things are limited opinions of others and have nothing to do with you. you can do what you desire and be as you wish to be at the age you want to be. the biggest driving force is love and the purpose of your actions, and when you are clear about your plan, you will achieve your dreams. and of course we will fail too, but it is just a stepping stone from which we can learn and excel next time. take care of your time.

qasim chauhan

万華鏡

mangekyou

kaleidoscope

enemy

i have seen people like you before, you are all like this. i don't want to be friends or talk to people like you. i will tell my child to not play with you. words like these are often used by people when they stereotype whole communities by just one person. here the enemy is 'the thought process' which is trained by society to generalize everything so easily. i am not saying you should start hating such people, but rather you should try to understand them. feel them from their perspective and then help them. if you tried enough, be kind to them and let them be. some battles are better not fought.

they are like this and doing these wrong things...but our way is better.... them vs. us, them vs. me... the over use of words like 'they', 'us' and 'me' is commonly seen in such people. here the problem is that they think they themselves are much better than other people, which gives them power to do or say nasty things to them. here the enemy is ignorance. such people don't really grasp the depth of diversity on this planet. we are all so different and yet connected. there are billions of species on earth and trillions of ideas. and there is nothing really good or bad, someone's good is others' bad and other's bad is someone's good. its perspective that matter. we need to embrace the diversity and love all cultures and communities. we are all a species on earth among million other species, so be kind to all species.

despite all the difference no one is really bad, its just our misunderstanding and lack of wisdom. ignorance is one of the prime reasons. once we all know the world and its uniqueness you'll value its magical realm.

tsū

pain

love and pain

love and pain are not very different from one another, and in most of cases, walk parallel to each other. but the wonderful thing about love is that love just colours pain into a painting of joy. one can be in pain, but suffering is optional when love is inside you. you can feel so sleepy, but for the love of your children or someone special your act of waking will make you more and more blessed with joy. suffering won't touch you if you choose love to be your companion. pain will be there, but it is just a small reminder and messenger on your journey.

do you remember how your mother stayed up many nights just so you can sleep well? do you remember how your father worked so hard through pain but still kept doing it because he wanted to give you joy?!! do you remember the days when you sacrificed your nights for your loved one?

love for others will help you see things more clearly. it will give you a deeper perspective in life. you can feel others and their pain. when i said love and pain are not very different i didn't mean love will bring you pain. it's that at first, pain is a teacher through which we learn love. through heartbreak we learn what love is. and once you've gone through this stage, you don't need pain to learn love. you can learn love and feel it in every emotion. once you feel connected with the universe and people, you will see love inside each person. we all want love and we all have seen pain, the path can be different but i wish every person to be healthy and kind to themselves and keep your love light shining bright like the sun. take care of yourself.

qasim chauhan

qasim chauhan

Made in the USA
Middletown, DE
25 June 2019